Beyond Pain: Coercing Violent Non-State Actors

Military strategy can no longer be thought of, as it could for some countries in some eras, as the science of military victory. It is now equally, if not more, the art of coercion, of intimidation and deterrence. The instruments of war are more punitive than acquisitive. Military strategy, whether we like it or not, has become the diplomacy of violence.[1]

INTRODUCTION

Suicide bombers are inspired and coached to their victims by al Qaeda and its franchises in Afghanistan, Iraq, Algeria, Yemen and beyond. Somali pirates disrupt shipping in the Indian Ocean, kidnapping civilians and extorting governments. Warlords terrorize the creeks of the Niger Delta as part of a "blood oil" trade. A quasi-religious drug cartel, La Familia, decapitates its way to control of Mexican drug trafficking routes. These violent non-state actors (VNSA), or armed groups, and others pervade the global conflict landscape. These conflicts pit nation-states against armed groups working to exploit, subvert and overthrow the international system; conflicts fueled by globalization's dark dynamics and punctuated by unconscionable violence against innocents; conflicts induced by true believers and hardened criminals armed with low- and high-tech weapons of mass destruction and disruption. In such conflicts, do we have options for using military force short of war? Are such adversaries susceptible to coercion? If so, how might a coercive strategy work?

This paper aims to answer these questions by examining the proposition that VNSA can be coerced by the threat or limited use of military force. I conclude that *coercion is a viable option for*

---

* Troy S. Thomas, Lt Col (Col Select) USAF, is a student at the National War College at the time of this writing. The views expressed in this paper are those of the author and do not necessarily reflect the official policy or position of the United States Department of the Air Force, National Defense University, Department of Defense, or the U.S. Government.

confronting VNSA. Even when leaders resist pressure, opportunities exist to induce change in the behavior of the organization and its support network. This said, coercion is exceptionally difficult, and the prospects for success are not promising. Hard does not equal futile. Coercion offers options when destroying the enemy is not desired or feasible, when diplomacy needs muscle, or when development takes too long to alter conditions.

Why do we need a study of coercion's utility now? Despite a persistent threat, contemporary theory and practice are not oriented on the VNSA problem. Focus remains on inter-state relations. One reason is a Cold War legacy of deterrence, associated with containment and preventing nuclear war. In the post-Cold War era, compellence emerged as a way to manage crises in the Balkans, Iraq, Afghanistan, Haiti and more. Second, deterrence was discarded early in the Global War on Terror (GWOT). In the wake of 9/11, the 2002 US *National Security Strategy* argued "deterrence will not work against a terrorist enemy…whose so-called soldiers seek martyrdom in death and whose most potent protection is statelessness."[2] By 2006, deterrence appeared headed to recovery. The US *National Strategy for Combating Terrorism* rejected coercion of "hard core" terrorists, but acknowledged its potential against terrorist networks.[3] It is not mentioned in the accompanying *National Military Strategic Plan for the War of Terrorism*.[4] In policy and practice, US strategy discounts coercion in favor of killing militants today and draining the support swamp tomorrow. As a consequence, we forfeit potential options in the strategic space between development and destruction.

The case for coercion is made by defining the problem, adapting strategy to the problem, and assessing the historical record. The problem is diagnosed in the second section. What are VNSA and why are they hard to coerce? In short, they are non-state organizations using violence. As such, our strategy is informed by understanding the behavioral dynamics common to all VNSA. Groups are the unit of analysis—e.g. terrorist groups, not individual terrorists or terrorism, are within the scope of this paper. Ruled out are spontaneous protests, lone actors, and non-governmental organizations that reject violence like multi-national corporations. Individuals are relevant to the extent they have a role in making or implementing the decisions of the group. Focus is not on movements, or ideologies. That said, ideology is central to an organization's resistance to coercion and its reasons for using violence. Extreme religious or nationalist groups, for example, are more able to neutralize coercive attempts.

The logic of coercion is adapted to VNSA in the third section. What are the ends, ways, and means? Coercion applies armed force to gain compliance by deterring or compelling adversary behavior. Given the inherent difficulty of proving whether coercion was decisive to a given outcome, the case for coercion must be based in part on the soundness of its logic in relation to what we know about how organizations really work. To test the conceptual logic, the fourth section examines a sub-set of the recent US record. What were the results, and to the extent our knowledge of the adversary allows, why?

The success rate is underwhelming. Nonetheless, we can improve the prospects for success by applying the lessons from a rigorous, but limited case history. Moreover, the specific case of coercing warlords in Somalia, 1992-1995, is analyzed to illustrate the effectiveness of coercion in light of these lessons. Thus armed, Section V concludes with recommendations for developing and implementing strategy for coercing VNSA.

As a preliminary introduction, coercion comes in two forms—deterrence and compellence.[5] Deterrence seeks to maintain the status quo by preventing an action before it occurs. Compellence seeks to reverse an action that has already occurred, or induce a different action. Both approaches work on the target's decision calculus by holding something of value at risk; coercion is directed at the adversary's will as opposed to destroying his capability. The contrast is best made by Nobel laureate Thomas Schelling in his classic *Arms and Influence*:

> There is a difference between taking what you want and making someone give it to you, between fending off assault and making someone afraid to assault you, between holding what people are trying to take and making them afraid to take it, between losing what someone can forcibly take and giving it up to avoid risk or damage. It is the difference between defense and deterrence, between brute force and intimidation, between conquest and blackmail, between action and threats. It is the difference between the unilateral, "undiplomatic" recourse to strength and coercive diplomacy based on the power to hurt.[6]

The power to hurt leverages potential force, or uses it in limited and discrete ways. As a result, the enemy retains the capacity for organized violence or illicit activity.

Advancing a viable coercive strategy is not a rejection of other instruments or approaches to gaining compliance. Economic, diplomatic and informational means can be brought to bear to sanction, contain and discredit. Sanctions and financial seizures, coupled with diplomatic isolation, can apply pressure to state and non-state actors. Law enforcement shares similarities with the military instrument, and is often the primary means of coercion domestically. Conversely, the instruments of power, including the military, can be used to motivate and reward behaviors through inducement and persuasion. In reality, military means are never used in isolation, or only to cause pain.

In terms of approaches, development mitigates the underlying conditions that give rise to violent groups. Public diplomacy engenders a less conducive environment while diplomatic negotiations facilitate compromise. Finally, coercion does not rule out warfighting. Make no mistake, coercion is violence. If it fails, wars may start. Destroying VNSA may be the preferred or only option. On the other hand, some VNSA cannot be eliminated, and domestic and international factors may constrain fighting in the near-term if at all. Rather than destroying the group, our political objectives may be satisfied if we can alter the behaviors of a surviving, less threatening group. In practice, all means and ways should be mobilized, sequenced, and integrated for success. To this end, military coercion is studied here to enable a comprehensive US grand strategy for confronting the VNSA problem.

PROBLEM

Non-state adversaries are not a new national security problem. The US was a rebel start-up, and our first decades involved coercive contests with Native American tribes and Barbary pirates. Modern armed groups pose challenges similar to their ancestors. Their decisions and behaviors seem irrational. When compared to states, they are harder to find, understand, signal, and pressure with military force. The VNSA may be elusive, but it is neither impenetrable nor impervious to pressure; they are social organizations made up of real people. By examining key organizational dynamics common to all VNSA, we can diagnose the problem in a way that guides tailored coercion of the leaders, organization, and affiliated supporters. Concurrently, we need to account for how the particular VNSA is using violence to counter coercion with coercion.

Real Rationality

State and non-state actors make imperfect decisions resulting in unexpected behaviors. This is contrary to the underlying premise of classical coercion theory, which assumes rationality of the target's decision calculus as well as behavior that "reflects purpose or intention."[7] Rather than dismissing VNSA choices as irrational and actions as random, we need to appreciate and anticipate their logic in its context.

When it comes to decisions, the rational actor makes consistent, value-maximizing choices from among a set of prioritized alternatives.[8] Several factors, posited by Nobel laureate Herbert Simon, temper this model: incomplete information; problem complexity; human computational limits; time constraints; and conflicting preferences among decision-makers.[9] Whereas we only need know the actor's goals to anticipate behavior using the rational model, Simon's "bounded rationality" requires us to "know the organism's goals, information and conceptualization it has of the situation, and its abilities to draw inferences from the information it possesses."[10] Bounded rationality applies to VNSA. Terrorism expert Bruce Hoffman argues "the terrorist is fundamentally a violent intellectual, prepared to use and indeed committed to using force in the attainment of his goals."[11] Going further, Robert Pape argues in *Dying to Win* that there is even a "strategic, social, and individual logic to suicide terrorism."[12] This logic applies at the individual level, but for our purposes, it is more important to note that the organization develops and manages the logic in a way to recruit and prepare individuals for suicidal attacks. The logic of suicide terrorism may be compelling, but it is rarely without skeptics in and out of the organization.

Real rationality also applies to behavior. Even with stringent internal control, individuals deviate from their roles and responsibilities. A delta always exists between what leaders want and the group does. For example, institutions behaved in ways inconsistent with leader preferences during the height of the 1962 Cuban Missile Crisis. An intercontinental ballistic missile (ICBM) was test launched by the Air Force, and the Navy communicated with Soviet nuclear submarines using depth charges.[13] Both sent mixed signals at a critical juncture. VNSA examples are less well-documented; however, it is not uncommon for suicide bombers to back out or guerrillas to defect. The formal structure never succeeds in conquering the informal social structure; behaviors emerge as a result of many individuals making choices based on multiple, and often incongruent motivations.[14] All actors are afflicted with real rationality.

Hard Targets

States are hard to coerce; non-state actors are harder. First, VNSA are harder to find. They do not usually have an address, preferring to operate in ungoverned spaces and through illicit networks—Al-Shabaab in Somalia.[15] To complicate matters, they also live on the Internet and prosper in modern, governed spaces—Aum Shinrikyo in Tokyo. Though elusive, the general location of most VNSA is known—Taliban in South Waziristan. In some cases, territory is actually ceded as in the Switzerland-sized sanctuary gifted to the Revolutionary Armed Forces of Colombia (FARC) by former President Andres Pastrana as part of a failed peace process.

Second, VNSA are harder to understand. Not only do they routinely change names—the Salafist Group for Call and Combat (GSPC) is now the al Qaeda Organization in the Islamic Maghreb—but their illegal status and secretive nature obscures answers to key questions: who decides; what do they value; what is their resolve; how do they judge costs and benefits; and how are decisions made and implemented? Sometimes we get partial answers from defectors and intercepted messages. A well-known example is a 2005 letter from al Qaeda's number two, Ayman al-Zawahiri, to its Iraq leader, Abu Musab al-Zarqawi, in which al-Zarqawi is cautioned against compromising long-term goals by sewing sectarian violence.[16]

Third, VNSA are harder to signal. Well-established means for communication and negotiation do not exist. In fact, dialogue with VNSA carries a strategic cost; it conveys legitimacy not always earned or desired. Direct dialogue; however, is common and often necessary. For example, the Good Friday accords brought peace in Northern Ireland only after years of controversial talks with senior leaders of the Irish Republican Army (IRA). When direct communication is not an option, indirect means exist through the media, intermediaries, or actions. For example, the US responded to the 1998 bombing of its Kenya and Tanzania embassies with cruise missile strikes against an al Qaeda training camp in Afghanistan and a suspected chemical facility—the Al Shifa pharmaceuticals plant and tannery—linked to Osama bin Laden in Sudan. Controversial and ineffective, the strikes were meant to signal US resolve and possibly deter future attacks.[17]

Fourth, VNSA are harder to pressure. In most cases, they have "fewer identifiable high value assets" that can be held at risk.[18] Some groups value their physical infrastructure and resources while others are willing to sacrifice people and things, but not ideas. Even if we identify value, the military may

5

not be the right tool due to lack of access and precision, or because the VNSA has a high pain threshold. VNSA resolve may also be stronger because "they have an asymmetrically higher stake in the outcome of the crisis or conflict."[19]

Organized Militants

VNSA are hardened, but not impenetrable targets. As a point of entry, VNSA are *non-state organizations that use collective violence*.[20] Each element of this definition has implications for how we understand and influence decisions and behaviors. It directs attention to the most relevant organizational dynamics for coercive strategy. It helps answer key questions about how armed groups develop, make decisions, control behaviors, relate to the environment and use violence for its own coercive purposes.

Not States

VNSA are not official entities or instruments of the nation-state. Although VNSA may serve as a state proxy, or be highly dependent on the resources provided by one or more states, they retain sufficient autonomy to make their own strategic choices. Hezbollah is a VNSA despite receiving direct support from Iran, whereas the Basij militia is an instrument of Tehran. As VNSA like Hezbollah in Lebanon, or Hamas in Gaza, integrate with and become government, they start losing non-state status. The line between state and non-state blurs, and the closer aligned the group is to a state, or the more governing responsibilities it assumes, the more susceptible it is to the logic of coercion.

The transformation from terrorist to president is just one manifestation of an organization's life-cycle. States have birthdays and evolve over time; however, VNSA are more transitory and prone to expand, regress, splinter, or die. Early on, the group struggles to survive by recruiting members and acquiring resources.[21] Choices are made by elites who are able to tightly control the use of violence primarily for symbolic or opportunistic reasons.[22] During growth, where most VNSA linger, formal structures elaborate, and sometimes splinter off, as leaders try to overcome "the idiosyncratic behaviors of group members."[23] Decision-making pressures grow as leaders seek to accommodate a wider array of stakeholders. Delegation widens the decision and action gap. At maturity, the VNSA gets closest to being a rational organization. Investment in people, resources, and policies creates value that is more susceptible to risk. With the stakes raised, the group has more resolve in the face of threats.

Social Organizations

VNSA are goal-directed social groups interacting with the environment.[24] The goals, stated or implied, reveal the organization's orientation to either a transcendental or transactional agenda. The former stresses ideology, religion, or some other existential code. Types include religious extremists such as al Jihad in Egypt, revolutionary Marxists such as the National Liberation Army (ELN) in Colombia, and ethnic nationalists such as the Basque Fatherland and Liberty (ETA) in Spain. These true believers are in the grip of a subjective reality that is highly resistant to external influence.[25] Because their agenda may be "divinely sanctioned," concerns over a low probability of success or loss of life are minimized.

In contrast, transactional VNSA live for money and power. These groups build and lose value more quickly. Defection is more likely if "profit or power is available elsewhere with acceptable risk."[26] The primary types are transitional criminal organizations (TCO) such as the Chinese Triads around the world, and warlords with private militias such as Thomas Lubanga of the Congo (now at the International Criminal Court). Other classifications exist; however, most are variations on these five main types. The most challenging VNSA are hybrids, leveraging pragmatic and normative agendas to expand their appeal, resources, and survivability.

Recognizing the limits of rational decision-making, coercion must nonetheless be informed by some knowledge of the actual decision process. In most social organizations, decisions result from a bargaining process involving a coalition of internal and external elites with their own constituencies, preferences, and sources of power.[27] Terrorism expert Brian Jackson argues that each party to the process will make choices based on beliefs about whether the proposed behavior: 1) positively influences relevant audiences; 2) advances group goals; 3) produces a positive internal reaction; 4) is worth the risk relative to alternatives; 5) will be sufficiently resourced; and 6) is based on "enough" information.[28] Coercion has a role to play in shaping each of these perceptions. Echoing an earlier insight, one of the most important implications of real-world decision-making, as assessed by Graham Allison, is that the "number of forks in the decision tree increases, independent actors multiply, and the prospect of the result achieving any precise original intent declines."[29]

Like all organizations, VNSA leaders expect their decisions to be implemented by group members who do not deviate from their assignments. Formal and informal communication pathways distribute the guidance, but it is by socializing members to the culture of the organization and maintaining a system of rewards and sanctions that role behaviors are enforced.[30] In a reflection of its transcendental agenda, the FARC still works to indoctrinate members to its Marxist ideology while at the same time relying on monetary incentives and corporal punishment to motivate performance.[31] All coercion strategies must overcome these two forms of internal resistance—socialization and sanctions.

At one time or another, all VNSA members operate at the group's boundary, linking it to an array of external stakeholders including states sponsors, operational enablers (financiers, smugglers, etc.), and affiliated groups (i.e. al Qaeda franchises).[32] This inter-organizational network represents a web of influence; most VNSA are dependent on others for sanctuary, money, recruits, intelligence, technology, weapons, and even legitimacy.[33] For example, Hamas receives weapons from Iran overland through Sudan and Egypt.[34] Osama bin Laden enjoyed sanctuary in Sudan until the US convinced Khartoum to expel him in 1996 through a combination of carrots and sticks.[35] Not to be forgotten, external players often have a say in decisions. Certainly state sponsors are key, but so are religious leaders and communities—preferences of the Irish Diaspora weighed on the IRA.[36] Not all stakeholders share the same level of commitment, nor are they all partners. The IRA provided weapons training to the FARC, but does not share its political ideology; and Pakistan is an enemy of al Qaeda, but has not been willing or able to go after its leaders in the remote Northwest Frontier Province. Consequently, external relationships often present lucrative targets for coercion as well as communication conduits to VNSA decision-makers. Of course, more self-sufficient and insular groups present fewer options.

Collective Violence

VNSA are distinguished by their deliberate use of violence. Knowing why violence is used is elemental to deterring further use or compelling a shift in use, possibly to alternative adversaries or even internally. Violence serves inter-related purposes. Internally, beatings and execution may be used to enforce role behaviors. Externally, it can serve to demonstrate potency, attract support, cause fear, and destroy opponents.

When directed externally, collective violence comes in three main forms: conventional, guerrilla, and terrorism.[37] According to insurgency and terrorism expert Bard O'Neill the forms are a "variety of organized violence emphasizing particular armed force, weapons, tactics and targets."[38] Historically, VNSA weakness relative to the state lends to emphasis on guerrilla warfare or terrorism, often in combination. There are notable exceptions where armed groups were able to field a conventional force, including Hezbollah, al Qaeda's 55th Arab Brigade, or the Liberation Tigers of Tamil Eelam (LTTE) before its defeat in 2009. To gain a conventional capability, the VNSA must overcome significant barriers to entry like access to physical space, weapon systems, and financial resources. Conventional strength comes with risk; the group actually becomes more vulnerable to coercion because 1) it now has forces that can be more easily put at risk, and 2) the state's asymmetric advantage in conventional force increases the probability that VNSA objectives will be denied.

In contrast, guerrilla warfare and terrorism are indirect approaches. As postulated by British strategist B. H. Liddell Hart, both take the path of least resistance in the physical sphere and least expectation in the psychological.[39] Guerrilla warfare avoids positional, force-on-force encounters. Rather, it involves "small-scale, limited actions, generally in conjunction with a larger political-military strategy, against orthodox military forces."[40] The guerrilla primarily targets government security forces and institutions in order to demonstrate their impotence and gradually erode the will of the state and populace.[41] Whereas the guerrilla generally avoids innocents to retain popular support, innocents are the victims of the terrorist. Victim selection is central to terrorism's heinous logic. Terrorism is violent theater; it creates and exploits fear to drive political change.[42] The normative violation associated with killing innocents in an abnormal way is intended to have a psychological impact on the actual target of the violence—the public, and ultimately the government. Terrorism, like guerrilla warfare, is coercion.

Summary

This section addressed the most relevant elements of a highly complex problem. Our quest for actionable insight requires us to first get past the rational actor assumption to a more realistic diagnosis. Decisions are the result of a bargaining process, and behaviors emerge from interactions by real people who deviate from their expected roles. Going further, VNSA on the whole are harder to find, understand, signal, and influence, particularly with armed force. By approaching them as social organizations, we can leverage insight to key organizational dynamics to frame and guide coercive strategy.

STRATEGY

Coercion is an approach to US grand strategy. It is a way military means can be applied in concert with non-military means in order to achieve political ends. Its logic was most fully developed into a rich body of theory during the Cold War. [43] Focus was on how to deter nuclear attack, contain the spread of communism, and compel changes in behavior by Third World states without triggering major power war. When the superpower rivalry waned, the theory was revised for application to so-called "rogue" states such as Iran, Libya, Iraq, and North Korea.[44] Objectives were to prevent regional aggression as well as weapons of mass destruction (WMD) development, proliferation and use. When the VNSA challenge is acknowledged in the literature, attention is deflected to states positioned to apply pressure. This section takes the next step—it adapts the conceptual logic of coercion directly to the VNSA problem. The case of coercion is strengthened if the ends, ways, and means of its logic can be connected to the key organizational dynamics identified in the last section.

Grand Strategy

The purpose of grand strategy, as articulated by Liddell Hart, is "to coordinate and direct all the resources of a nation, or band of nations, towards the attainment of the policy object of war...."[45] Its setting is war in the broadest sense as an engagement among actors involving the threat or use of force. It applies to the entire conflict spectrum from nuclear to conventional to irregular war. Its jurisdiction extends beyond warfighting to war preparation and conflict prevention as well as war termination and recovery. As argued by Edward N. Luttwak, grand strategy "includes the highest level of interaction between any parties capable of using force against each other, including terrorist and criminal groups."[46] In contemporary terms, grand strategy equates to US national security strategy.

Grand strategy has an inherent logic: resources (means) are applied (ways) in order to achieve desired results (ends). Means include all sources of hard and soft power, mobilized as diplomatic, informational, military, and economic instruments. Power and its instruments serve the national security objectives, or ends, of the state.[47] Ways are a strategic approach that interrelates means to ends through a concept(s) for how to integrate and sequence the application of available capabilities. Coercion is such a concept—it describes how military means can be applied to improve the prospects for gaining compliance with our demands short of war.

Ends

Ends let us know if grand strategy succeeds or fails. They are the political objectives to which the military goals are subordinate. *Compliance is the minimalist end of coercion.* Compliance only requires that the desired behavior occurs even when such behavior is not in the interest or a preference of the VNSA—believe what you want, but do what we say.[48] Compliance is more reliable when it results from deliberate decisions carried out faithfully by group members. While not preferred, our previous analysis suggests compliance may also be obtained even when the leadership does not intend it due to coercion's effect on other stakeholders in and out of the organization. Ideally, the leaders choose to comply, even if reluctantly, but modest goals may be satisfied with this lesser form of compliance.

When compliance equals inaction, it is deterrence. Different action is compellence—stop doing something, or do something else. The latter is more difficult to achieve since it seeks to alter the status quo. As put by Schelling, "'Do nothing is simple," "do something" ambiguous. "Stop where you are" is simple; "go back" leads to "how far?'"[49] As a consequence, deterrence is easier to communicate and more promising for goals such as do not adopt violent methods, attack us, or pursue WMD. In contract, compellence goals must specify when, where, and how much.[50] This imposes a communication burden if, for example, we want the group to stop something underway like cocaine trafficking or do something new like relocate. In practice, reversing a complete action versus deterring a future action is rarely a clear-cut division.[51]

As our demands increase, compliance is less likely to be a sufficient objective. VNSA are unlikely to foreswear violence, give up territory, or abandon their agenda if the main stakeholders do not perceive the outcome as being in their interest. For these ambitions, we need to go beyond compliance to cooperation and conversion. Cooperation is in play when the group concludes that compliance is consistent with their interests and preferences. A loftier goal, conversion, occurs when the VNSA completely restructures its beliefs, attitudes, and perceptions—believe what we say, then behave accordingly.[52] For these ends, coercion is rarely sufficient; other ways and means must be brought to bear.

Even if the desired behavior results, it is difficult to know whether coercion was the cause, particularly for deterrence. It is easier to spot failure. According to Robert Pape in *Bombing to Win*, the criteria for failure are simple:

Coercion fails when the coercer stops its coercive military actions prior to concessions by the target, when the coercer's attacks continue but do not produce compliance by the target, or when the coercer imposes its demands only after complete defeat of the target.[53]

War is often evidence of failed coercion. Conversely, qualified success can be claimed when behavior conforms to our demands even if the reasons are unclear. We are most successful, according to Byman, when "the adversary gives in while it still has the power to resist."[54]

Ways

Ways describe how we achieve compliance by applying means. Compellence and deterrence represent the broad ways of coercion; however, distinctions fade as we get into the mechanics of influencing the adversary's calculus of costs and benefits through combinations of punishment and denial. Just as compliance may be an insufficient end, coercion is usually not a sufficient way. Inducement and persuasion are essential, mutually supporting approaches.

Decision Calculus

The logic of coercion starts simple—costs outweigh the benefits of not complying—and gets complicated quickly.[55] VNSA stakeholders calculate the relationship among costs and benefits within their bounded decision context. The two main costs of not complying are punishment and denial of objectives. But complying also has a price. Internal and external pressures for action, to mount one more spectacular terrorist attack, can be significant. Mature, transcendentalist groups like Jemaah Islamiya in Southeast Asia are driven by religious duty underpinned by perceived injustice. Or, in cases like ETA in Spain, sustained operations are necessary to prove the group's vitality. Costs of complying are usually greater in deterrence situations, at least in the near-term.[56] Doing nothing carries less risk to the group's support base or sense of honor than does altering behavior. The principal benefit of complying is group survival, or to a lesser extent, assurances that punishment is not forthcoming and long-term goals remain viable. Benefits of not complying also exist, including enhanced prestige and cohesion for the group, and monetary rewards, promotion or spiritual validation for individuals.

Of course, the calculus is not clear and perceptions of value trump "real" costs and benefits every time.[57] A sense of how much the VNSA values the behavior indicates resolve. The jihadist, seized by religious duty, values the fight more than the pirate seeking to score another high seas ransom.[58] Value is also assigned to costs and benefits; disruption of a weapons proliferation network may be less threatening than a loss of safe haven. The available options have value too—attack, do not attack, attack later, attack a different target, and so on.[59] Finally, we must overcome the human tendency to discount the future even though an on-going relationship is expected. According to Robert Art, "imagined future pain hurts less than present pain."[60] Therefore, the VNSA will value sunk costs more highly and take more risk to preserve a current position than enhance it.[61]

Credibility is required to shape perceptions about value and the probability that costs or benefits will be imposed. Not only must our resolve be believable, but the target must believe that the threat can be executed—that the cost will actually result.[62] In general, deterrence is more credible. The negative objective—do nothing—expects less of the coercer. Returning to Schelling, deterrence is stage-setting: "by announcement, rigging the trip-wire, by incurring the obligation—by waiting."[63] Action is up to the VNSA; the coercer only acts if the wire is tripped. Deterrence cedes the initiative. Compellence takes it by initiating an "action (or an irrevocable commitment to action) that can cease, or become harmless" when the VNSA responds.[64] It often requires a demonstration of force to gain credence. For the demonstration to have its intended effect, it must be accompanied by a clear communication of purpose through relevant channels.

Punish and Deny

On the whole, the coercer is less able to manipulate benefits.[65] Therefore, we return to cost imposition through punishment and denial as the primary ways of deterring or compelling. Punishment threatens pain and damage to something of value to the VNSA. It works when the VNSA complies, not because its strategy is thwarted, but because the costs are too great.[66] Direct punishment, underway in overseas contingencies formerly known as GWOT, entails a range of obvious ways to inflict pain: seizing assets, denying sanctuary, killing and imprisoning personnel, exposing illicit activities, and more. Cumulatively, these efforts isolate the VNSA from its external support network and generate internal dissention, defection, and role deviation to widen the decision-action gap. Indirect punishment strengthens our partners through security cooperation and military diplomacy while undermining external support to the VNSA. Punishment's utility decreases when it comes to damaging intangible values such as group's worldview. As a final caution, if the pain reaches existential proportions, group resolve will strengthen to the degree survival is threatened—it is possible to over punish.

Given the difficulty of locating something to credibly punish, particularly for transcendentalist groups, denial has better prospects. It threatens the VNSA by denying capability, opportunity, and objectives.[67] Denial is offensive when it degrades capability to conduct operations and illicit activity. In this respect, it looks like punishment. Denial is more evident in defensive measures to generate uncertainty and reduce vulnerabilities. It denies opportunity by protecting potential victims and preventing target access. An active defense in depth across all domains (air, space, land, sea, cyber) trades space for time in order to characterize and respond to the specific threat. Attribution is a prerequisite for initiating a coercive engagement; general coercion may still be possible, but coercion of specific group requires identification. Layered defenses further complicate "adversary's attack planning and execution and may require adversaries to undertake more complex and visible operations."[68]

Measures to secure ports, conduct biometric surveillance, or harden critical infrastructure may lead the terrorist to "look elsewhere or to change (delay or defer) their decisions to act."[69]

Denial of objectives is a counter-coercion approach that is oriented against the adversary's strategy, and may hold the greatest promise for confronting VNSA. It is predicated on understanding and disrupting the end-ways-means logic of the VNSA's strategy. It also hinges on interrupting the intended psychological chain reaction associated with the group's use of collective violence. To this end, we should aim to impact VNSA target and method selection, and consider how our response relates to their logic and narrative. In particular, it is important to dampen and undercut the psychological reaction the terrorist seeks. Strong defenses, rapid recovery, and decisive, but not excessive retribution can mitigate fear and embolden a resilient target audience, primarily US communities and government. Denial is likely to be more effective against armed groups with transactional goals early in their development; however, it can also contribute to discrediting the ideology or narrative of mature transcendental groups who need success to demonstrate potency or divine authority.

Induce and Persuade

There are non-military ways to coerce, and for coercion to have better odds, it must be integrated with inducement and persuasion. Even when not vulnerable to military means, VNSA may respond to diplomatic, economic, and informational coercion. The logic is the same, but the methods differ. Ways of political coercion involve conveying legitimacy on a rival, breaking off negotiations, or gaining endorsement from an intergovernmental organization like the United Nations (UN). Aggressive diplomatic campaigns—such as those against Somalia's warlords and Bosnia's ethno-nationalists—are a necessary component to all coercive attempts. Economic coercion entails the disruption, seizure, or manipulation of critical financial resources. This too has its limits. Based on a study of their use, Richard Haas contends that "sanctions almost always result in some economic hardship, but this impact is often insufficient or unable to force the desired political change...."[70] Finally, informational coercion threatens the veracity of VNSA claims now as a means to discredit their narrative later.[71] Proactive public affairs can be used to contest embellishment and conspiracy with facts while public diplomacy can shape perceptions over the long haul.

Inducement flips the logic of coercion, and is critical when we want cooperation or conversion. It increases the benefits of compliance or reduces the costs of non-compliance.[72] The benefits go beyond withholding pain to incentives and facilitation. Incentives involve concessions and compensation, such as lifting sanctions or providing safe haven, diplomatic recognition, and money.[73] Facilitation reduces the cost of compliance, usually by providing a missing capability.[74] In this respect, security is often needed to protect against rejectionists, or logistics for movement to negotiations and out of conflict zones. For inducement to work it must avoid appeasement and violating policies regarding official exchanges with a VNSA, particularly terrorist groups.

The third form of influence is persuasion. Whereas coercion and inducement manipulate costs and benefits, persuasion aims to alter "the decision context in which costs and benefits of various options are weighed."[75] In terms of the rhetoric of persuasion, diplomacy has primacy, and every agency and instrument can impact VNSA decision-making by introducing new values and options, or in a more fundamental way, reframing the issue.[76] Whether undertaken through direct negotiations or radio broadcasts, efforts to shape perceptions, attitudes, and beliefs require a credible authority appealing to the reason and emotion of the intended audience.[77] Within the context of strategic communications, military psychological and deception operations can isolate the adversary and insulate the public from its coercive strategy.[78] Regardless of approach, consistency in word and deed is the most powerful form of persuasion.

Means

Coercion needs the military, but wants the integrated and synchronized use of all instruments of power. Overwhelming military power is not the answer. First, coercion involves limited force by definition. Going big contradicts our declared aim of altering behavior without destroying the group. Second, threats of nuclear retaliation, invasion, or massive conventional attack lack credibility. Third, it is rarely effective. Coercive contests are more about balancing intentions than capabilities.[79] The key questions are not about inventories, but about 1) threshold—how much pain or how little success to tolerate, and 2) expectation—what will happen next. Therefore, follow-through with right-sized capabilities has greater resonance.

Intelligence and communications underpin all approaches. Effective multi-discipline intelligence is needed to find VNSA, attribute behaviors, and understand decisions and actions. Military diplomacy, public affairs, and psychological operations facilitate a complicated public and private discourse with all stakeholders. The heavy lifting of direct punishment is done by precision strike, cyber attack, and special operations to seize, disrupt, and damage. Intelligence, surveillance, and reconnaissance (ISR) capabilities expose groups and attribute behaviors. For indirect punishment, a host of means strengthen our partners" ability to counter VNSA: foreign internal defense, security sector reform, foreign military sales, military education and training, and other forms of security cooperation.[80] All capabilities that contribute to a multi-domain defense are relevant to a denial strategy. Emphasis should be on early detection and attribution, critical vulnerability protection, and resilient forces, infrastructure, and communities.[81]

Summary

VNSA are appropriate targets for a coercive strategy—the logic applies. Compliance with our demands is the minimum requirement. The primary ways of coercion, deterrence, and compellence shape an opponent's perception of costs and benefits relative to other options through integrated punishment and denial. Rarely sufficient, inducement and persuasion are mutually supportive ways that draw on military and non-military capabilities.

RECORD

Coercion is a high risk, low probability approach. It costs blood and treasure, and fails more than it succeeds. Failure is obvious when the adversary does not comply, but the reasons for success are hard to discern. As a consequence, the number of case studies focused on coercion short of war is limited. This is despite a history of coercion dating to the Peloponnesian Wars, when the Athenian generals infamously asserted, "the strong do what they can and the weak suffer what they must."[82] If we zoom in on the US experience, coercion was used in many of the hundred-plus military interventions since our founding. Insight to why coercion worked can be drawn from the entire historic ledger; however, this section focuses on a sub-set of more recent cases in which the US was a primary coercer. The lessons from these cases are then tested against a specific VNSA case—intervention in Somalia, 1992-1995. Building on previous sections, we now look to real-world experience to illustrate the viability of a coercive strategy and derive lessons for how to improve its prospects during implementation.

Sober Results

Coercion works about a third of the time. This is the conclusion of seven cases examined by Alexander George in *Forceful Persuasion* and eight different cases studied in *The United States and Coercive Diplomacy*, edited by Robert Art and Patrick Cronin.[83] Six of the fifteen involve VNSA. Three directly tackle the VNSA problem—Somalia, Bosnia, al Qaeda. VNSA are party to the Laos, Nicaragua, and Kosovo cases. The following survey does not do justice to their complexity. Rather, it is intended to provide a brief context for the lessons that apply to states as well as non-state actors.

Failure

The US did not achieve its overall aims in seven of fourteen cases: Japan, Vietnam, North Korea, Iraq, Kosovo, al Qaeda, and Somalia. VNSA are central actors in the last three. Starting with WW II, the Japanese attack on Pearl Harbor followed years of miscalculation based on inconsistent signals and entrenched positions on both sides of the Pacific.[84] Arguably, the US oil embargo was heavy-handed economic coercion that underestimated Japan's motivation and lacked corresponding inducements. Going further, George suggests that we caused too much pain: "Pearl Harbor is not a simple case of deterrence failure. It is, rather, a case in which coercive diplomacy provoked the adversary into a decision for war."[85]

Advancing to Vietnam 1965, the US attempted to coerce North Vietnam into suspending its support to the Viet Cong in South Vietnam. Operation Rolling Thunder steadily increased strategic bombing of military forces and logistics infrastructure in the North with high value-targets in Hanoi and Haiphong off limits. George argues strategic bombing failed to coerce Hanoi because it lacked strength, a sense of urgency, and real compromise.[86] Robert Pape sees it differently: "The denial model was impotent because air power could not thwart Hanoi's guerilla strategy" and it failed to hold the civilian population at risk.[87] In sum, it failed to punish—not enough pain—and deny sufficiently.

Fast forward to the 1990s. In the midst of crisis on the Korean peninsula in 1994, an Agreed Framework emerged to halt North Korea's nuclear program. It resulted from 1) inducements of direct dialogue with the US (as well as other aid and economic benefits), 2) threats to seek UN sanctions and take military action, and 3) a dramatic, unauthorized diplomatic mission by former President Jimmy Carter that aborted the downward spiral in relations.[88] While seemingly successful, it was violated as early as 1997 with a uranium enrichment program that was disclosed in 2002. An unreliable opponent, lack of US options, and insufficient pressure by external stakeholders, particularly China, are among the many culprits.

Six distinct coercion attempts were tried with Iraq between 1990 and 1998. Although scored a failure due primarily to Saddam Hussein's ability to survive and subvert punishment, the analysis suggests a "qualified success" within the context of an overall deterrence strategy.[89] As one example, Hussein deployed two Republican Guard divisions to the Kuwait border in October 1994, threatening a potential invasion. In response to an ultimatum from President Bill Clinton and the deployment of 170 aircraft and over 6,500 personnel, he withdrew the forces. On the other hand, he was not compelled to withdraw from Kuwait in 1991, and massive air strikes against suspected WMD facilities in 1998 did not compel him to cease a cat and mouse game with the United Nations Special Commission (UNSCOM) over suspect WMD programs.

Kosovo in 1999 is considered a coercion failure because an air war was ultimately carried out by the North Atlantic Treaty Organization (NATO) to gain concessions from Serbian leader Slobodan Milosevic. Moreover, NATO had trouble coercing the non-state Kosovo Liberation Army (KLA), not because the KLA lacked value to put at risk, but because it was not party to negotiations at Rambouillet, and it was a competitor to NATO's main partner in Kosovo.[90] Milosevic's ultimate capitulation is generally attributed to the escalation in bombing, threat of a ground offensive, allied interest in a negotiated settlement, a shift in Russian position against Serbia, and concessions to withdraw a roadmap to Kosovo independence.[91]

Finally, US coercive attempts against terrorism in the 1990s consisted primarily of criminal prosecutions and occasional, limited military operations such as the cruise missile attacks against al Qaeda-linked targets in Sudan and Afghanistan in 1998. These coercive measures and others (restricting travel, financial seizures, etc.) were insufficient to prevent the 1993 and 2001 World Trade Center bombings, the 1998 attack on US embassies in Kenya and Tanzania and several other attacks including the USS Cole in Yemen and the Pentagon. According to terrorism expert, Martha Crenshaw, coercive attempts failed because 1) the enemy was hard to identify and understand, 2) al Qaeda and its operations were never at risk, 3) it was difficult to credibly threaten escalation, and 4) there was no sense of urgency until after 9/11.[92] Like this study, her analysis assumes al Qaeda is an organization that has tangible and intangible value that can be held at risk. Consistent with our understanding of transcendentalist VNSA during growth, al Qaeda was and remains highly resistant to coercion.

Not Sure

Mixed results were obtained on three occasions—Nicaragua, Libya, and Taiwan Strait. Beginning in 1981, the US aimed to contain and later destabilize the Soviet-backed, Sandinista regime in Nicaragua by backing the Contra rebels. The Contras are an example of a VNSA being used as a proxy to coerce a state. After eight years of stalemate, and in the shadow of the Iran-Contra affair, the approach only served to stimulate strong domestic opposition and a remarkable effort by Central American leaders to insulate the Daniel Ortega regime.[93] The confrontational approach was abandoned for carrots and sticks that included $50 million to sustain the Contra deterrent along with agreement to abandon efforts to overthrow the Sandinistas by force.[94] As a result, the Soviet Union halted military supplies, and elections were held, resulting in a "stunning ideological defeat for communism."[95]

The second mixed result comes from efforts to coerce Libya to end support for terrorism in the 1980s while signaling resolve to all state sponsors, particularly Iran and Syria. In the wake of an April 1986 West Berlin discothèque bombing, the US executed an air raid against Libyan installations to include Muammar al-Gaddafi's headquarters.[96] Support for terrorism declined initially, suggesting success until the tragic bombing of Pan Am 103 in 1988 killed 270 innocent people. Two Libyan officials were tried and convicted. Shifting tactics, a series of carrots (lifting sanctions), and sticks (implied threat stemming from the US war in Iraq) ultimately led Libya to forswear terrorism in 1999 and surrender its WMD program in 2003.

In the 1996 Taiwan Strait crisis, it is not clear whose coercive attempt worked. To dissuade Taiwan's apparent move toward independence, Beijing test-fired several missiles close to the island.[97] The US responded by positioning two aircraft carrier battle groups in the Strait. This escalation was a deterrent against Chinese military action, and a compellent to de-escalate Beijing's policy toward Taiwan.[98] The crisis was defused, and China refrained from further military action. On the other hand, Taiwan did not declare independence. Most likely, Taipei's restraint was a response to both domestic and external pressures.

Success of Sorts

Success can be reasonably claimed in four cases: Laos, Cuba, Bosnia, and Haiti. Laos and Bosnia involved VNSA with multiple state sponsors in each case. In 1961, newly elected President John F. Kennedy used coercion to check Pathet Lao guerrilla advances while scaling back US commitment to the Royal Lao government. The effort was complicated because the Soviet Union, China, and North Vietnam all differed in the perception of costs, benefits, and risk.[99] To communicate resolve, Kennedy moved forces to Thailand and "ordered the four hundred US „civilian advisors" to put on their military uniforms and join Royal Lao army units on the front line."[100] As inducement, he offered disengagement in exchange for a neutral Lao. Initially rejected, a ceasefire and weak coalition government eventually resulted.

Only a few months later, Kennedy was in a stand-off over the deployment of Soviet medium-range ballistic missiles to Cuba. Compellence was attempted through several inter-related approaches 1) diagnose and publicly expose the threat with ISR, 2) implement a naval blockade, 3) threaten air strikes and invasion by posturing forces, 4) opening back-channel dialogue for a negotiated solution, and 5) provide a delayed inducement of removing US missiles from Turkey. Despite the stakes, neither Kennedy nor Soviet leader Nikita Khrushchev "engaged in reckless competition in risk-taking but acted cautiously to avoid escalation."[101] By limiting ends and means, the missiles were withdrawn and global nuclear war was avoided.

Before Kosovo, and in the wake of the Yugoslavia's dissolution, the US participated in UN and NATO efforts to coerce peace in Bosnia-Herzegovina from among three ethno-nationalist VNSA with strong ties to state sponsors: Bosnian Muslims, Croats, and Serbs. Without detailing them all, there were at least five US attempts to compel Bosnian Serb behavior to include releasing the "strangulation" of Sarajevo.[102] A stalemated conflict facilitated compliance by the Bosnian Serbs, which was also consistent with their desire to "keep alive negotiations for a comprehensive cease-fire" to lock in their gains.[103] Milosevic was motivated to exert pressure on the Bosnian Serbs by limited air strikes and the potential of sanctions being lifted. The comprehensive coercive strategy led to a complicated and tenuous peace.

With twenty-five thousand troops ready to invade in September 1994, Haitian dictator Raoul Cedras conceded to return power to the duly elected former president, Jean-Bertrand Aristide. In the moments before his deadline, Cedras was ready to call "Clinton's bluff—he's chickenshit, there's no congressional support, no public support—and as the big-bad-wolf rhetoric escalated, American credibility became inextricably braided in the process."[104] For three years prior, Cedras and his cronies prospered despite an economic embargo of an already impoverished state, and they muted multiple threats to include turning away the USS *Harlan County* with its contingent of UN police advisors in October

1993.[105] In the end, it took independent negotiators with unsurpassed credibility—Jimmy Carter, Sam Nunn, and Colin Powell—to orchestrate the dramatic moment of capitulation.

Lessons

These cases and others suggest several lessons for increasing the prospect of achieving our aims. As a result of George's analysis, success is more likely for states and VNSA when the following conditions are met: 1) clarity and consistency in what is demanded; 2) stronger motivation than the adversary; 3) a sense of urgency; 4) adequate domestic and international support; 5) adversary fear of unacceptable escalation; and 6) clarity concerning the terms for settling the crisis.[106] Perceptions of value and risk are paramount. All the factors do not need to be present for success; however, it is essential that

> an asymmetry of motivation operates in favor of the coercing power, that it is really time-urgent to respond to the coercing power's demands, and that the opponent must take seriously the possibility that the coercing power will engage in escalation that would pose unacceptable costs.[107]

Art and Cronin endorse these determinants of success, adding that the odds of are further enhanced when 7) positive inducements are offered, 8) less, not more is demanded of the target, and 9) military force is threatened or used in a denial, not a risk of punishment, mode.[108] Together, these nine lessons are consistent with the conceptual logic of coercion. They should guide US coercion strategy with an understanding that the specific type of VNSA, our goals, and the overall context shape which combination of factors is most relevant in a given contest.

Somalia

Somalia is a lucrative case for analyzing coercion of VNSA for several reasons. First, it was an early post-Cold War test for the UN. It marked the first time Chapter VII enforcement provisions of the UN Charter were invoked for internal conflict. Second, its complexity was compounded by multiple players: VNSA; nation-states; inter-governmental organizations (IGOs); and non-governmental organizations (NGOs).[109] From among these, the defining contest pitted the UN and US against rival Somali factions: the Somali National Alliance (SNA) led by Mohamed Farah Aideed and dominated by the Habr Gedir sub-clan, and the United Somali Congress (USC) led by Ali Mahdi Mohamed and dominated by the Abgal sub-clan.[110] Each faction had its own organizational structure, sub-groups, and alliances. Notably, the VNSA are not state-sponsored; however, both rely on illegal arms shipments and other activities for financial support. Third, its three distinct phases supports intra-case comparisons: 1) UN Operations in Somalia I (UNOSOM I), Apr—Dec 1992; 2) United Task Force (UNITAF), Dec 1992—Apr 1993; and 3) UNOSOM II, May 1993—Mar 1995. The phases, or rounds, provide a framework for assessing the effectiveness of coercion in light of the determinants of success.

UNOSOM I

Round one opened with the establishment of UNOSOM I by Security Council Resolution (UNSCR) 751 on 24 April 1992. Coercion was not central to generating the shaky ceasefire agreement on which intervention was predicated. When attempted, it was not able to protect distribution of relief supplies to four million people in urgent need.

Armed force proved inadequate to punish or deny, and the threat of escalation was not taken seriously. Fifty peacekeepers deployed to Mogadishu immediately, and an additional 500 followed in September. The warlords acquiesced because the small number of blue helmets, operating under restrictive Article VI rules of engagement, did not threaten their power.[111] To make sure, they laid siege to the outgunned Pakistanis, who refused to leave the airfield while mercenary Somali "technicals" looted and extorted NGOs.[112] Concurrently, twenty US Air Force C-130 sorties per day delivered 28,000 tons of aid during Operation Provide Relief; however, US forces did not protect distribution.[113] Responding to the anarchy, UN Secretary General Boutros Boutros-Ghali gained approval to deploy another 3,000 peacekeepers, threatening Chapter VII enforcement if they were not accepted. Ali Mahdi embraced the plus-up while Aideed viewed it as lethal. Instead of reducing violence to forestall their arrival, he retorted: "If you send in blue helmets, you might as well send coffins in with them, we're going to kill them for their berets and boots alone."[114]

Though constrained in use, the military instrument was coupled to a proactive diplomatic effort by UN Special Envoy, Ambassador Mohamed Sahnoun. In his words, he "pursued a strategy of putting the clan system to work for Somalia."[115] Direct, routine meetings with Aideed, Ali Mahdi, and local elders paved the way for peacekeepers and sustained a fragile ceasefire. The restraint obtained between the SNA and USC did not translate into reduced criminal activity, and Sahnoun was undermined by his NY headquarters. For example, his credibility collapsed when news of the 3,000 plus-up was received with surprise in Mogadishu over BBC radio; Aideed's suspicion of UN motives seemed to be confirmed. Sahuoun later resigned, and his replacement's less active approach was no match for the deteriorating situation.[116]

Inducements were introduced out of sequence prior to the peacekeepers and ineffectively paired to the coercive attempt. Humanitarian relief was meant to save lives and encourage political settlement by arresting the crisis. Instead, the aid strengthened the warlords who stole on behalf of merchants desperate for food stocks.[117] Predation was further facilitated when distribution points were set-up in areas they controlled. Even though problems were recognized by the UN, innovative options such as a monetization plan advocated by Sahuoun and Andrew Natsios of USAID were stillborn. Their strategy was designed to bypass the warlords and energize the market by auctioning low-price, high-value food items to merchants while distributing low-value food aid for free.[118]

Round one went to the warlords. The UN gained compliance to introduce peacekeepers who were then unable to protect relief distribution. The aid was in turn exploited by warlords at the people's expense. An initially active, hands-on diplomatic approach held promise, but was undermined by inconsistent policy, insufficient muscle, and counterproductive inducements.

UNITAF

Round two opened with passage of UNSCR 794 on 3 December 1992, authorizing a US-led Chapter VII peace enforcement operation. Coercion was central to securing relief distribution; overwhelming force was married to consistent, credible diplomacy and inducements. As put by US Special Envoy to Somalia, Ambassador Robert Oakley, "our purpose would be achieved by dialogue and cooption, using implicit threats of coercion to buttress requests for cooperation among the factions and with UNITAF."[119]

UNITAF rapidly inserted 38,000 forces from 20 countries, including the 28,000 US personnel of Operation Restore Hope. Preceded by Oakley's warnings, and backed by an impressive show of force in Iraq, UNITAF quickly established military primacy. An early, exemplary use of force helped. As recounted by the Marine commander, Major General Wilhelm, in the first days "a Fiat armored car and a technical vehicle took a couple of random shots at a helicopter, and we speared both the vehicles in the streets of Mogadishu."[120] Message received. Overmatched, the principal antagonist—Aideed—and his allied warlords exercised restraint. Given UNITAF's short tenure, they could also afford to wait as long as their power was not fundamentally threatened by disarmament.

The willingness to use force was synchronized in policy and practice by aggressive diplomacy in pursuit of objectives narrowly defined by President George Bush: "open the supply routes, to keep the food moving, and to prepare the way for a UN peace-keeping force...."[121] Partnering with the UNITAF commander, General Robert Johnston, Oakley pursued a strategy of "plucking the bird." He paired "frequent and friendly consultations" with marginalization to weaken the warlords "one feather at a time."[122] A national reconciliation process was kick-started; however, there was no attempt to impose political settlement.[123] Oakley's deputy, Jeffrey Herbst, framed the political process as an incentive, imploring the warlords to seize "a once in a lifetime opportunity" to rebuild their country.[124] Implementation was strengthened through daily meetings of a joint security committee at a neutral site. Further progress was undermined by warlord intransigence, which was compounded by a major policy disconnect between the UN in New York and Washington over disarmament and mission expansion.[125]

Although the mandate did not include nation-building, UNITAF's Deputy for Operations, Brigadier General Anthony Zinni, acknowledged: "We did creep outside our mission a lot."[126] Troops built or repaired over 1,200 km of roads and bridges, dug wells, and established schools, orphanages, and hospitals.[127] Monetization was finally initiated, but success was limited by hoarding and control over the markets by warlords. On the other hand, massive profits were an incentive for continued compliance. Security provided the space to initiate civil administration and a Somali police force within the context of an energized political process. For the first time, the informational instrument was activated for persuasion. US Army psychological operations distributed leaflets and produced the "Rajo," meaning "Hope" in Somali, newspaper and radio broadcast.[128]

Round two went to the United States. Warlord compliance reflected a sensible decision calculus based on being no match for coalition firepower, deriving massive profits from relief distribution, and waiting for the mission"s expiration in April 1993. Arguably, UNITAF"s short-lived success invited overreach in round three.[129]

UNOSOM II

Round three opened with passage of UNSCR 814 on 26 March 1993, expanding the UNOSOM II mandate to nation-building and disarming all factions.[130] Coercion failed to check the escalation in violence after UNITAF"s abrupt departure due to insufficient military means and incoherent diplomacy. Reacting to attacks on UN forces attributed to Aideed, UNSCR 837 was passed on 6 June 1993 to direct "all necessary measures" against the SNA.[131] Not one to cower, Aideed became more aggressive. In the wake of "Blackhawk Down," UNOSOM II retreated from war, relying on anemic coercion until the end.

UNOSOM II never commanded more than 16,000 peacekeepers, which included 3,000 US logistics personnel. As part of the deal to withdraw US forces, newly elected President William Clinton agreed to leave a 1,150 Quick Reaction Force from the 10th Mountain Division under a separate US command. With fewer and less capable forces, UNOSOM II was charged with securing twice the territory. The warlords quickly exploited the transition and perceived weakness, moving crew-served weapons out of impound to confront UN forces. When 24 Pakistanis were killed in June, the hunt for Aideed was on, and civilians were caught in the crossfire. Near misses by the newly introduced Task Force Ranger culminated in the ruinous 3 October raid, leaving 18 US Army Rangers dead and others in captivity. Aideed"s legend grew, UNOSOM"s credibility suffered, and the US was headed to the exit.

The political gains made in the March Addis Ababa peace conference were not sustainable in light of the changed security situation and inconsistent diplomacy. Political leadership passed from Oakley to the UN"s new Envoy, retired Admiral Jonathon Howe, who struggled to overcome distrust of the UN. By this time, Aideed concluded that the peace process and disarmament policy were existential threats. The conflict turned personal; Howe placed a $25,000 bounty on the "caged scorpion"s" head.[132] Aideed replied with a $1 million bounty on Howe. Seeking to forestall a descent to war, the Clinton administration countered the UN position, shifting policy away from the manhunt toward a diplomatic solution. Unfortunately, word of the change did not reach Task Force Ranger before the ill-fated October raid.

With security collapsing, plans to rehabilitate the economy and civil administration withered. The incentive of relief aid, so often counterproductive, was less relevant due in part to mitigation of the famine"s worst effects. Focus shifted to returning refugees and providing health care, potable water, and food security. As with UNOSOM I, much of the heavy lifting was by NGOs in part because logistics, engineers, and medical personnel exited with UNITAF. From Howe"s perspective, "I felt we had a big mismatch.... We just begged and borrowed people right and left to be able to manage, even inadequately."[133] Momentum on building a 10,000 Somali National Police Force also collapsed due to a lack of funding.[134] Finally, the plug was pulled on a key means of persuasion with the termination of UNITAF psychological operations.

Round three went to Aideed. A seam-filled transition and weaker UN invited his challenge. Coercion gave way to a personalized war for which the UN lacked the means and will to win—the motivation asymmetry continued to favor Aideed. Instead, Aideed used coercion to restore the UN/US policy of negotiation; his rivals were weakened and his bargaining position reached a zenith.

Assessment

The Somalia experience reveals that credible armed force is a necessary, but insufficient means—other instruments of power must be brought to bear. Moreover, coercion is a necessary, but insufficient way—inducement and persuasion must be integrated. In round one, skilled diplomacy was unable to overcome deficient and often counterproductive military and economic means. In round two, muscular diplomacy, organized and oriented on narrow goals, was tightly coupled to inducement and persuasion using economic and informational means. UNITAF gained temporary compliance—lives were saved. In round three, a weaker force and disjointed policy were exploited by the warlords. Aideed, in particular, succeeded in coercing the coercer. His overall success reflects an asymmetry of motivation in his favor. Not only did the UN and US not consistently present a credible threat of escalation, but they were not able to sustain domestic and international support for the operation. Coercion worked, but only during the brief period of UNITAF when the nine lessons were applied.

Summary

The record indicates coercion against states and VNSA mostly fails, but success is possible and more likely when the lessons identified here are applied. Moreover, the lessons from coercive attempts against states translate to the VNSA problem. More directly, the odds of success increase as the demands narrow. Prospects further improve when credible military means are coupled with non-military instruments to persuade and induce. To this end, skilled diplomacy is needed to ensure clarity and consistency in what is demanded as well as coherent terms for resolving the conflict.

CONCLUSION

As developed in this study, the rationale for rehabilitating coercion in national security and military strategy is three-fold. First, VNSA are not irrational actors immune to pressure. They are social organizations that decide and behave in ways that can be understood and influenced. Second, the logic of coercion applies to VNSA. Compliance with our preferred behaviors can be achieved by shaping perceptions of costs and benefits; however, we must appreciate coercion's limits and its unique application to armed groups. Third, the limited case analysis of coercive attempts against VNSA suggests it can work when several conditions are working in our favor. Even though the prospects for success are limited, coercion may be the best or only option. When feasible, there are at least nine main consequences for adopting it as part of a counter-VNSA strategy. Although the strategy process is never linear, the consequences suggest a certain sequence for developing, integrating, and implementing coercion.

1) *Diagnose the problem.* As social organizations, VNSA are open to investigation and engagement even though they are harder to find, understand, signal, and pressure. By focusing on the organizational dynamics common to all groups, a basic appreciation for how the VNSA decides and behaves can be discerned. In general, groups that integrate a transcendental and transactional agenda are more resistant to pressure, particularly those embracing extreme ethno-nationalist or religious convictions. Groups early in their life-cycle have less to hold at risk than those at maturity, particularly when the group takes on governing responsibilities. Decisions emerge from a bargaining process that reflects bounded rationality within their context. Behaviors emerge as well that are rarely a true reflection of the decision. Insight to these dynamics provides a general sense of coercion's feasibility as well as opportunities for pressuring specific groups.

2) *Choose narrow goals.* The more we demand, the less successful we will be. A minimalist approach that focuses on compliance with specific demands is best. Demands to do nothing—deterrence—are generally easier for a VNSA to accommodate than demands to do something different—compellence. It is not necessary to change attitudes or beliefs, but only the perception of costs and benefits relative to the available options. It is sufficient to gain the behavior we want even if the group does not share our preferences. Once we adopt goals that fundamentally threaten a group's source of power or existence, coercion's utility is lost.

3) *Aim at the organization.* Compliance can be obtained without altering the decision calculus of the group's leadership. Certainly, it is preferable if our coercive strategy can influence the decisions of leaders who in turn impose the decision on the organization. Leaders, or more specifically stakeholders to the decision process, are a priority target for coercion. But, coercion should also target sub-groups,

24

classes of individuals, and even individuals within the organization. In many cases, inducing deviation from assigned roles may be sufficient to get the behavior, or lack of behavior we seek. Just as importantly, our strategy must attend to external stakeholders on whom the VNSA depends. In many cases, they do not share the same level of commitment to the group"s agenda. A multi-level approach aimed at the whole system is more likely to generate the net effect of coercion even when elites prove resistant.

4) *Communicate clearly, consistently.* Coercion is communication. For the threat or limited use of force to be credible, our demands, the costs of non-compliance, and the benefits of compliance must be articulated, transferred, received, and processed in the way we intend. Of course, we must admit and anticipate the inherent limitations to effective communication. To this end, our signaling should leverage the medium and media most relevant to the VNSA to include using external stakeholders with access to the organization. Moreover, it is imperative that our actions appear consistent with our rhetoric. When military force is used, it must be what George refers to as "exemplary." That is, the use of force is symbolic; it should be just enough of the right kind to send the message. It must also be demonstrative of what is to come if compliance does not closely follow its use.

5) *Deny always, punish selectively.* Given the inherent difficulties of coercing VNSA, our ability to punish is limited. In general, VNSA are highly resistance to pain even if we can find something of value to hurt. Of course, we can impose some pain by killing or capturing group members, taking away sanctuary, or cutting off critical resources. That said, the record suggests this is hard to do and rarely gains compliance. Therefore, we must get beyond the pain caused by punishment to the psychological pain caused by denial. A strategy that counters the VNSA strategy by denying opportunity and objectives is better. In this regard, defense is stronger than offense. Moreover, it focuses on what we can control—how we respond. Based on our understanding of why the VNSA uses collective violence, we can act to neutralize the psychological chain reaction that is essential to their strategy. By countering their strategy, we undermine their appeal, and ultimately, their reason for being.

6) *Induce and persuade.* Coercion rarely works on its own. Success correlates well with inducements. This means offering a clear pathway to settling differences, and including incentives to motivate movement down the path. Persuasion is linked to communication, but also incorporates the idea of working to shape the decision context. That is, a credible authority can appeal to reason and emotion to introduce new options and encourage different perceptions regarding costs. Persuasion can run in parallel to coercion; but according to the analysis of Art and Cronin, positive inducements have their greatest effect when offered after threats are made.[135] Inducement and persuasion also provide opportunities to integrate non-military means.

7) *Plan for the future*. Coercion is not a discrete event at a given moment in time. It is a contest that extends into the future. In fact, it is the expectation that the relationship will continue that enables coercion to work. Therefore, a coercive strategy must consider the implications for subsequent rounds of interaction. If compliance does not follow from our initial demand, what next? After an exemplary use of force that fails to alter behavior, what next? To avert an unwanted transition to war, our strategy must have a clear idea for how settle to the conflict and a plan for how to control escalation.

8) *Be motivated*. Coercion is a contest of wills. Before initiating a coercive attempt, we must judge our motivation to implement threats. The failure to follow through is a death blow to credibility, which is certain to result in a worse situation than when the crisis started. Once it is clear that the adversary's motivation exceeds ours, and if we are not willing to escalate further, we need to transition away from a coercive strategy quickly and credibly.

Coercion is a viable option for confronting VNSA. The threatened, or limited use of force short of war should be part of a comprehensive strategy that integrates defense, diplomacy and development to prevent the emergence, influence the behavior, and if necessary, defeat non-state adversaries. If we choose coercion, and if it fails, we must be ready for war.

BIBLIOGRAPHY

Allard, Kenneth. *Somalia Operations: Lessons Learned.* Washington, DC: NDU Press, 1995.

Allison, Graham and Philip Zelikow. *Essence of Decision: Explaining the Cuban Missile Crisis.* NY: Longman, 2nd ed., 1999.

Art, Robert and Patrick Cronin, editors. *The United States and Coercive Diplomacy.* Washington, DC: United States Institute of Peace, 2003.

Atkinson, Rick. "Marines Close Curtain on U.N. in Somalia; Final Departure Ends Quest to Rid Country of Famine, Anarchy." *Washington Post.* March 3, 1995.

Asprey, Robert B. *War in the Shadow: The Guerrilla in History.* Garden City, NY: Doubleday & Company, Volume 1, 1975.

Auerswold, David P. "Deterring NonState WMD Attacks." *Political Science Quarterly.* Winter 2006/2007.

Baker III, James A. *The Politics of Diplomacy: Revolution, War and Peace 1989-1992.* NY: G. P. Putnam's Sons, 1995.

Billington's, James H. *Fire in the Minds of Men: Origins of Revolutionary Faith.* NY: Basic Book Publishers, 1980.

Boutros-Ghali, Boutros. *The United Nations and Somalia, 1992-1996.* NY: UN Department of Public Information, 1996.

Byman, Daniel. *Trends in Outside Support for Insurgent Movements.* Santa Monica, CA: RAND Corporation, 2001.

Clarke, Walter and Jeffrey Herbst, editors. *Learning from Somalia: The Lessons of Armed Humanitarian Intervention.* Boulder, CO: Westview Press, 1997.

Clausewitz, Carl von. *On War.* Edited and translated by Michael Howard and Peter Paret. Princeton, NJ: Princeton University Press, 1984.

Coll, Steve. *The Secret History of the CIA, Afghanistan, and bin Laden, from the Soviet Invasion to September 10, 2001.* NY: Penguin Press, 2004.

Cooper, Drury. *Economic Sanctions and Presidential Decisions: Model of Political Rationality.* Gordonsville, VA: Palgrave Macmillan, 2006.

Cragin, Kim and Scott Gerwehr. *Dissuading Terror: Strategic Influence and the Struggle Against Terrorism.* Santa Monica, CA: RAND Corporation, 2005.

Crocker, Chester A. "The Lessons of Somalia: Not Everything Went Wrong." *Foreign Affairs.* 1995.

Daft, Richard L. *Organization Theory and Design.* Mason, OH: South-Western, 2004.

Davis, Paul K. and Kim Cragin Jackson, editors. *Social Science for Counterterrorism: Putting the Pieces Together*. Santa Monica, CA: RAND Corporation, 2009.

Davis, Paul K. and Brian Jenkins. *Deterrence and Influence in Counterterrorism*. Santa Monica, CA: RAND Corporation, 2002.

Dobbins, James, John G. McGinn, Keith Crane, Seth G. Jones, Rollie Lal, Andrew Rathmell, Rachel M. Swanger, and Anga R. Timilsina. *America's Role in Nation-Building: From Germany to Iraq*. Santa Monica, CA: RAND Publications, 2002.

George, Alexander and Richard Smoke. *Deterrence in American Foreign Policy: Theory and Practice*. NY: Columbia University Press, 1977

George, Alexander. *Forceful Persuasion: Coercive Diplomacy as an Alternative to War*. Washington, DC: United States Institute of Peace Press, 1991.

George, Alexander, David K. Hall and William E. Simons. *The Limits of Coercive Diplomacy: Laos, Cuba, Vietnam*. Boulder, CO: Westview Press, 1994.

Haass, Richard and Meghan L. O'Sullivan. *Honey and Vinegar: Incentives, Sanctions, and Foreign Policy*. Washington, DC: Brookings Institution Press, 2000.

Hirsch, John L. and Robert B. Oakley. *Somalia and Operation Restore Hope: Reflections on Peacemaking and Peacekeeping*. Washington, DC: US Institute of Peace Press, 1995.

Hoffman, Bruce. *Inside Terrorism*. NY: Columbia University Press, 1998.

Johnson, David E., Karl P. Mueller, and William H. Taft, Jr. *Conventional Coercion Across the Spectrum of Operations: The Utility of U.S. Military Forces in the Emerging Security Environment*. Santa Monica, CA: RAND Corporation, 2002.

Katz, Daniel and Robert L. Kahn. *The Social Psychology of Organizations*. NY: John Wiley and Sons, 2nd ed., 1978.

Lahneman, William J., editor. *Military Intervention: Cases in Context of the Twenty-First Century*. NY: Rowman & Littlefield Publishers, Inc., 2004.

Laqueur, Walter. *The New Terrorism: Fanaticism and the Arms of Mass Destruction*. NY: Oxford University Press, 1999.

Liddell Hart, B.H. *Strategy*. NY: Praeger Publishers, 1967.

Luttwak, Edward N. *Strategy: The Logic of War and Peace*. Cambridge, MA: Belknap Press, 2001.

Menkhaus, Ken and Louis Ortmayer. "Key Decisions in the Somalia Intervention." *Pew Case Studies in International Relations*. Washington, DC: Institute for the Study of Diplomacy, Georgetown University, 1995.

Naim, Moises. *Illicit: How Smugglers, Traffickers, and Copycats are Hijacking the Global Economy*. NY: Doubleday, 2005.

Oakley, Robert B. "An Envoy's Perspective." *Joint Force Quarterly*. Autumn 1993.

Oberdorfer, Don. *The Two Koreas: A Contemporary History*. Reading, MA: Addison-Wesley, 1997.

O'Neill, Bard E. *Insurgency and Terrorism: Inside Modern Revolutionary Warfare*. Washington, DC: Brassey's Inc., 1990.

Pape, Robert. *Bombing to Win: Air Power and Coercion in War*. Ithaca, NY: Cornell University Press, 1996.

Pape, Robert. *Dying to Win: The Strategic Logic of Suicide Terrorism*. NY: Random House, 2005.

Poole, Walter S. *The Effort to Save Somalia, August 1992—March 1994*. Washington, DC: Joint History Office, 2005.

Post, Jerold M. "Psychological Operations and Counterterrorism." *Joint Force Quarterly*. Issue 37, 2nd Quarter 2005.

Post, Jerold. *The Mind of the Terrorist: The Psychology of Terrorism from the IRA to al-Qaeda*. NY: Palgrave Macmillan, 2007.

Rosegrant, Susan. "A „Seamless" Transition: United States and United Nations Operations in Somalia." *Kennedy School of Government Case Program*. 1996.

Sahnoun, Mohamed. *Somalia: Missed Opportunities*. Washington, DC: US Institute of Peace Press, 1994.

Schaub, Gary. "Deterrence, Compellence, and Prospect Theory." *Political Psychology*. Vol. 25, No. 3, 2004.

Schelling, Thomas. *Arms and Influence*. New Haven, CT: Yale University Press, 1966.

Shacochis, Bob. *The Immaculate Invasion*. NY: Viking, 1999.

Shafritz, Jay M. and J. Steven Ott, editors. *Classics of Organization Theory*. NY: Harcourt College Publishers, 2001.

Simon, Herbert. "Human Nature in Politics: The Dialogue of Psychology with Political Science." *American Political Science Review 79*, 1985.

Snyder, Glenn H. "Deterrence and Power." *The Journal of Conflict Resolution*. Vol. 4, No. 2, June 1960.

Strassler, Robert. Editor, *The Landmark Thucydides: A Comprehensive Guide to the Peloponnesian War*. NY: The Free Press, 1996.

Thomas, Troy, Steve Kiser and William Casebeer. *Warlords Rising: Confronting Violent Non-State Actors*. Lanham, MD: Lexington Books.

Tilly, Charles. *The Politics of Collective Violence*. Cambridge, UK: Cambridge University Press, 2002.

US. *The National Security Strategy of the United States of America*. Washington, DC: Whitehouse, 2002.

US. *The National Strategy for Combating Terrorism*. Washington, DC: Whitehouse, September 2006.

US. *National Military Strategic Plan for the War on Terrorism*. Washington, DC: Joint Chiefs of Staff, 2006.

US European Command. *Military Contribution to Cooperative Security Joint Operating Concept*. Washington, DC: The Joint Staff, 19 September 2008.

US Joint Forces Command. *Strategic Communications Joint Integrating Concept*. Washington, DC: The Joint Staff, 19 September 2008.

US Northern Command. *Homeland Defense and Civil Support Joint Operating Concept*. Washington, DC: The Joint Staff, 2007.

US Special Operations Command. *Irregular Warfare Joint Operating Concept*. Washington, DC: The Joint Staff, 11 September 2008.

US Strategic Command. *Deterrence Operations Joint Operating Concept*. Washington, DC: The Joint Staff, Version 2.0, 2006.

Viotti, Paul R., Michael Opheim and Nicholas Bowen, editors. *Terrorism and Homeland Security: Thinking Strategically about Policy*. Boca Raton, FL: CRC Press, 2008.

ENDNOTES

[1] Thomas Schelling, *Arms and Influence* (New Haven, CT: Yale University Press, 1966), 34.

[2] *The National Security Strategy of the United States of America* (Washington, DC: Whitehouse, 2002), 15.

[3] *The National Strategy for Combating Terrorism* (Washington, DC: Whitehouse, September 2006), 11.

[4] *National Military Strategic Plan for the War on Terrorism* (Washington, DC: Joint Chiefs of Staff, 2006).

[5] Variations on compellence, used throughout this paper, include coercive diplomacy, forceful persuasion and armed suasion.

[6] Schelling, *Arms*, 2-3.

[7] Graham Allison and Philip Zelikow, *Essence of Decision: Explaining the Cuban Missile Crisis* (NY: Longman, 2nd ed., 1999), 16.

[8] Ibid., 18.

[9] Allison, *Essence*, 20, and Mary Jo Hatch, *Organization Theory* (NY: Oxford University Press, 1999), 274.

[10] Herbert Simon, "Human Nature in Politics: The Dialogue of Psychology with Political Science," *American Political Science Review 79* (1985): 294. Quoted in Allison, *Essence*, 20. An appreciation of values and norms, which are a function of culture and ideology, is also relevant.

[11] Bruce Hoffman, *Inside Terrorism* (NY: Columbia University Press, 1998), 43.

[12] Robert Pape analyzed data for 315 suicide attacks between 1980 and 2003, concluding that suicide terrorism has an internal logic that links the suicide attacks with strategic objectives. *Dying to Win: The Strategic Logic of Suicide Terrorism* (NY: Random House, 2005), 1, 7.

[13] Allison, *Essence*, 234-239.

[14] The disconnect between the formal, mechanistic and informal, dynamic organization is address by Philip Selznick, "Foundations of Organization Theory," in *Classics of Organization Theory*, edited by Jay M. Shafritz and J. Steven Ott (NY: Harcourt College Publishers, 2001), 125-127. The foundational theory of multiple motivations and determinants of behavior is provided in the same collection by Abraham Maslow, "A Theory of Motivation," 174-175, taken from *Psychological Review*, 50 (1943).

[15] For excellent study of global illicit networks, see Moises Naim, *Illicit: How Smugglers, Traffickers, and Copycats are Hijacking the Global Economy* (NY: Doubleday, 2005).

[16] Full transcript released by the Director of National Intelligence on 11 October 2005, available at: www.dni.gov/press_releases/20051011_release htm.

[17] Martha Crenshaw, "The Response to Terrorism," in *The United States and Coercive Diplomacy*, edited by Robert J. Art and Patrick M Cronin (Washington, DC: US Institute for Peace Press, 2003), 326-327.

[18] US Strategic Command (USTRATCOM), *Deterrence Operations Joint Operating Concept (JOC)* (Washington, DC: The Joint Staff, Version 2.0, 2006), 18.

[19] Ibid., 17.

[20] Troy Thomas, Steve Kiser, and William Casebeer, *Warlords Rising: Confronting Violent Non-State Actors* (Lanham, MD: Lexington Books, 2005), 9.

[21] Richard L. Daft, *Organization Theory and Design* (Mason, OH: South-Western, 2004), 325.

[22] For a thorough examination of the dynamics of collective violence, see Charles Tilly, *The Politics of Collective Violence* (Cambridge, UK: Cambridge University Press, 2002).

[23] Thomas, *Warlords*, 116.

[24] Daft, *Organization*, 11.

[25] For an examination of non-religious, "revolutionary" agendas, see James H. Billington's classic, *Fire in the Minds of Men: Origins of Revolutionary Faith* (NY: Basic Book Publishers, 1980).

[26] Thomas, *Warlords*, 122.

[27] Hatch identifies this as a coalition model of decision-making, *Organization*, 277-278. Graham describes it in detail as the "governmental politics paradigm" in *Essence*, 255-324.

[28] Brian A. Jackson, "Organizational Decisionmaking by Terrorist Groups," in *Social Science for Counterterrorism: Putting the Pieces Together*, edited by Paul K. Davis and Kim Cragin (Santa Monica, CA: RAND Corporation, 2009), 221-232.

[29] Allison, *Essence*, 288.

[30] Daniel Katz and Robert L. Kahn, *The Social Psychology of Organizations* (NY: John Wiley and Sons, 2nd ed., 1978), 52-54.

[31] Interview on 17 November 2009 with William Wood, US Ambassador to Colombia, 2003-2007. Also see, Walter Laqueur, *The New Terrorism: Fanaticism and the Arms of Mass Destruction* (NY: Oxford University Press, 1999), 212-215.

[32] A variety of useful classifications exist. Paul Davis and Brian Jenkins propose the following: internal (top leaders, lieutenants, foot soldiers, recruiters) and external (suppliers, states supporters, populations, other sources of moral and religious support). *Deterrence and Influence in Counterterrorism* (Santa Monica, CA: RAND Corporation, 2002), 15. Deterrence expert Brad Roberts recommends a similar structure for the problem of WMD Terrorism: jihadi foot soldiers, leaders, professionals, affiliate groups, state sponsors, operational enablers, moral legitimizers, and passive state enablers. "Deterrence and WMD Terrorism: Calibrating its Potential Contributions to Risk Reduction," Institute for Defense Analysis Paper 4231 (June 2007): 11.

[33] Hatch, *Organization*, 65. For an excellent analysis of the criticality of external support to insurgencies, see Daniel Byman, *Trends in Outside Support for Insurgent Movements* (Santa Monica, CA: RAND Corporation, 2001).

[34] Aron Heller, "Israel: Commandos seize huge Iranian arms shipment," Associated Press, 4 November 2009.

[35] For a full account, see Steve Coll, *The Secret History of the CIA, Afghanistan, and bin Laden, from the Soviet Invasion to September 10, 2001* (NY: Penguin Press, 2004), 325.

[36] Jerold Post, *The Mind of the Terrorist: The Psychology of Terrorism from the IRA to al-Qaeda* (NY: Palgrave Macmillan, 2007), 53.

[37] Bard E. O'Neill, *Insurgency and Terrorism: Inside Modern Revolutionary Warfare* (Washington, DC: Brassey's Inc., 1990), 33-37.

[38] Ibid., 24. The forms are distinct from strategic concepts for war such as insurgency, revolutionary war, *jihad*, limited war, etc. Each of these political-military approaches to war is likely to involve one of more of the forms of violence.

[39] B. H. Liddell Hart, *Strategy* (NY: Frederic A. Praeger, 1968), 341.

[40] Robert B. Asprey, *War in the Shadow: The Guerrilla in History* (Garden City, NY: Doubleday & Company, Volume 1, 1975), xi.

[41] O'Neill, *Insurgency*, 36.

[42] Leading terrorism expert, Bruce Hoffman, defines terrorism as "the deliberate creation and exploitation of fear through violence or the threat of violence in the pursuit of political change." *Inside Terrorism,* 43. Bruce Jenkins introduced the idea of terrorism as theater in his chapter, "International Terrorism: A New Mode of Conflict," in *International Terrorism and World Security*, edited by David Carlton and Carlo Schaerf (London: Croom Helm, 1975), 16.

[43] The era's most prominent theorists include George Kennan, Thomas Schelling, Herman Kahn, and Bernard Brodie.

[44] Alexander George, Daniel Byman, Robert Pape, Lawrence Freedman, and others did the intellectual heavy-lifting in the 1990s.

[45] Hart, *Strategy*, 335.

[46] Edward Luttwak, *Strategy: The Logic of War and Peace* (Cambridge, MA: Belknap Press, 2001), 201.

[47] Strategy conforms to Carl von Clausewitz's contention that war's purpose is to attain the political aims of the sovereign. Clausewitz argues the "political object—the original motive for the war—will thus determine both the military objective [ends] to be reached and the amount of effort it requires [ways]." *On War*, edited and translated by Michael Howard and Peter Paret (Princeton, NJ: Princeton University Press, 1984), 81.

[48] Kim Cragin and Scott Gerwehr, *Dissuading Terror: Strategic Influence and the Struggle Against Terrorism* (Santa Monica, CA: RAND Corporation, 2005), 15.

[49] Schelling, *Arms*, 72.

[50] Ibid., 72.

[51] Daniel Byman and Matthew Waxman, *The Dynamics of Coercion* (NY: Cambridge University Press, 2002), 6-7.

[52] Cragin, *Dissuading*, 19.

[53] Robert Pape, *Bombing to Win: Air Power and Coercion in War* (Ithaca, NY: Cornell University Press, 1996), 15.

[54] Byman, *Dynamics*, 3.

[55] Byman and Waxman contend, "Coercion should work when the anticipated suffering associated with a threat exceeds the anticipated gains of defiance." Ibid., 10.

[56] Gary Schaub draws on expected utility theory to argue that in many cases deterrence is actually easier than compellence. "Deterrence, Compellence, and Prospect Theory," *Political Psychology*, Vol. 25, No. 3 (2004): 389.

[57] Ibid., 10.

[58] For a discussion of suicide bomber motivation and resolve, see Pape, *Dying to Win*, 89-92.

[59] The Deterrence Operations JOC introduces the related idea of "consequences of restraint." Accordingly, "Encouraging adversary restraint plays a critical role in deterrence operations because adversary decision-makers weigh the benefits and costs of acting *in the context of* their expectations of what will happen if they do not act." USSTRATCOM, 27.

[60] Robert Art, "Coercive Diplomacy: What do we know?," *The United States*, 363.

[61] Byman, *Dynamics*, 12.

[62] Schelling, *Arms*, 35.

[63] Ibid., 72.

[64] Ibid., 72.

[65] Pape, *Bombing*, 16.

[66] Art, "Coercive Diplomacy," 362.

[67] James Smith and Brent Talbot, "Terrorism and Deterrence by Denial," in *Terrorism and Homeland Security: Thinking Strategically about Policy*, Paul R. Viotti, Michael Opheim, and Nicholas Bowen, editors (Boca Raton, FL: CRC Press, 2008), 53. Also see David E. Johnson, Karl P. Mueller, William H. Taft, Jr., *Conventional Coercion Across the Spectrum of Operations: The Utility of U.S. Military Forces in the Emerging Security Environment* (Santa Monica, CA: RAND Corporation, 2002), 16-17. For discussion of denial as it relates to terrorist and criminal organizations, see David P. Auerswold, "Deterring NonState WMD Attacks," *Political Science Quarterly*, 121, 4 (Winter 2006/2007).

[68] US Northern Command (USNORTHCOM), *Homeland Defense and Civil Support JOC* (Washington, DC: The Joint Staff, 2007), 19-20.

[69] Ibid., 56.

[70] Richard Haass and Meghan L. O'Sullivan, *Honey and Vinegar: Incentives, Sanctions, and Foreign Policy* (Washington, DC: Brookings Institution Press, 2000), 2. See also Drury Cooper, *Economic Sanctions and Presidential Decisions: Model of Political Rationality* (Gordonsville, VA: Palgrave Macmillan, 2006).

[71] Stories connect actions to a symbolic framework and a narrative thread that arcs through history. The narratives of many terrorists groups, for example, present an interpretation of past and current events that is not only dramatically different from the strategic communications of the United States, but that is effective at discrediting our message while motivating others to violent action. The more compelling narrative often wins, particularly when it embraces the elements of rhetoric and good storytelling. In our narrative competition with al Qaeda and associated jihadist organizations, we face master storytellers like Osama bin Laden and Ayman al-Zawahri. Not only are they perceived as credible to a broad Muslim public, but their rhetoric appeals to both the rational and emotional.

[72] US Joint Forces Command (USJFCOM), *Strategic Communications Joint Integrating Concept (JIC)* (Washington, DC: The Joint Staff, 19 September 2008), 76.

[73] In response to the 1990 Taureg rebellion in Mali, for example, the government combined limited military action with political decentralization and economic investment to resolve the conflict. The result was the Accords of Tamanrasset, 6 January 1991. This case is examined in full by Kalifa Keita, Lieutenant Colonel, Malian Army, "Conflict and Conflict Resolution in the Sahel: The Tuareg Insurgency In Mali," Report of Strategic Studies Institute, Carlisle Barracks, PA (1 May 1998): 79.

[74] Gary Schaub, "Power and Influence," Powerpoint Presentation, Air War College, February 2007.

[75] USJFCOM, *Strategic Communications JIC*, 79.

[76] Schaub, "Power and Influence." For a comprehensive discussion of the military's role in persuasion, see USJFCOM, *Strategic Communications JIC*.

[77] Effective persuasion is story-telling. Good stories will be consistent in rhetoric and deed. Really good stories employ all the elements of rhetoric as well as a rich cast of characters, a protagonist and antagonist, and a physical and mental trial for the protagonist. Effective rhetoric involves credibility (ethos), appeal to reason (logos), and appeal to emotion, or affect (pathos). When our story is presented by officials lacking credibility, or the message fails to anticipate emotional responses, it is likely to fall on deaf ears and may generate frustration or rage.

[78] See Jerold M. Post, "Psychological Operations and Counterterrorism," *Joint Force Quarterly*, Issue 37 (2nd Quarter 2005): 105-110.

[79] Glenn H. Snyder, "Deterrence and Power," *The Journal of Conflict Resolution*, Vol. 4, No. 2 (June 1960): 165.

[80] For a complete discussion see, US Special Operations Command (USSOCOM), *Irregular Warfare JOC* (Washington, DC: The Joint Staff, 11 September 2008), and US European Command (USEUCOM), *Military Contribution to Cooperative Security*, (Washington, DC: The Joint Staff, 19 September 2008).

[81] The full set of required military capabilities is discussed in USNORTHCOM, *Homeland Defense JOC*.

[82] The quotation is from the Melian Dialogue. Robert Strassler, editor, *The Landmark Thucydides: A Comprehensive Guide to the Peloponnesian War* (NY: The Free Press, 1996), 352.

[83] Iraq 1990-1991 is covered in both studies. Moreover, Somalia and Iraq can actually be broken down into 8 distinct coercive attempts. Of note, the cases focus on compellence; however, deterrence is inherent to all. Art, "Coercive Diplomacy," 381. While other case studies are available, this set is highly regarded, and it uses a fairly consistent intellectual framework to enable comparative analysis. Alexander George and Richard Smoke examine nine additional cases in *Deterrence in American Foreign Policy: Theory and Practice* (NY: Columbia University Press, 1977). Also referenced, Alexander George, *Forceful Persuasion: Coercive Diplomacy as an Alternative to War* (Washington, DC: US Institute for Peace, 1991).

[84] George, *Forceful Persuasion*, 22-23.

[85] Ibid., 21.

[86] Ibid., 44-46.

[87] Pape, *Bombing to Win*, 195.

[88] William Drennan, "North Korea," in Art, *The United States*, 195. See also Don Oberdorfer, *The Two Koreas: A Contemporary History* (Reading, MA: Addison-Wesley, 1997), 305-336

[89] Jon Alterman, "Iraq 1990-1998," Ibid., 298-299. An example of a success is Operation Vigilant Warrior, which involved the rapid deployment of US forces to the region in 1994 in response to Iraq"s deployment of two Republican Guard divisions to the Kuwait border. Iraq ultimately withdrew its forces.

[90] Steven Burg, "Bosnia and Kosovo," in Art, *The United States*, 103.

[91] Ibid., 103.

[92] Martha Crenshaw, "The Response to Terrorism," in Art, *The United States*, 346.

[93] George, *Forceful Persuasion*, 51.

[94] James A. Baker III, *The Politics of Diplomacy: Revolution, War and Peace 1989-1992* (NY: G. P. Putnam"s Sons, 1995), 58.

[95] Ibid., 60.

[96] The raid, known as Operation El Dorado Canyon, killed 45 government personnel and 15 civilians including Gaddafi"s adopted daughter.

[97] Robert Ross, "The 1995-96 Taiwan Strait Confrontation," in Art, *The United States*, 257.

[98] Art, "Coercive," 382-383.

[99] George, *Forceful Persuasion*, 27.

[100] Ibid., 29.

[101] Ibid., 34. See also Allison, *Essence*.

[102] Burg, "Bosnia," 58.

[103] Ibid., 62.

[104] Bob Shacochis, *The Immaculate Invasion* (NY: Viking, 1999), 34.

[105] Robert A. Pastor, "Haiti, 1994," in Art, *The United States*, 125.

[106] George, *Forceful Persuasion*, 80. George actually breaks motivation out into two separate, but related factors. These factors also proved themselves in nine separate cases covered with Richard Smoke in *Deterrence*. Not addressed here is strong leadership, which is introduced in a separate study by George, David K. Hall, and William E. Simons, *The Limits of Coercive Diplomacy: Laos, Cuba, Vietnam* (Boulder, CO: Westview Press, 1994).

[107] Ibid., 81.

[108] Art, "Coercive," 391.

[109] States like Kenya and the US had key roles outside participation in a UN organization. IGOs included the Organization of African Unity (OAU), League of Arab States (LAS), and Organization of the Islamic Conference (OIC). According to USAID Assistant Administrator Andrew Natsios, approximately 24 NGOs were engaged. Of these, the International Committee of the Red Cross (ICRC) was critical. Susan Rosegrant, "A „Seamless" Transition: United States and United Nations Operations in Somalia," *Kennedy School of Government Case Program* (1996): 10. Other VNSA include criminal gangs not tied to the main political factions as well as the possible involvement of the Islamic Union (El Itihad El Islami).

[110] Boutros Boutros-Ghali, Secretary-General of the United Nations, "Introduction," *The United Nations and Somalia, 1992-1996* (NY: UN Department of Public Information, 1996), 11-12.

[111] Chapter VI of the UN Charter allows for force in clear cases of self-defense. Available at www.un.org/en/documents/charter/chapter6.shtml.

[112] Poole, *The Effort*, 11. According to Rosegrant, "To rent a „technical"—one of the ubiquitous Land Rovers…with their tops sliced off and machine guns mounted on them—might cost $100 a day, while the gunmen…demanded about $500 a month." "Technical" dervies from the NGO practice of itemizing the leasing of such vehicles on expense reports under "technical assistance." "A „Seamless" Transition," 6.

[113] Figures from Kenneth Allard, *Somalia Operations: Lessons Learned* (Washington, DC: NDU Press, 1995), 35. Of note, NGOs were equally if not exceeding this amount through independent means.

[114] Attributed to Aideed by Assistant Secretary of State for International Organization Affairs, John Bolton, in Rosegrant, "A „Seamless" Transition," 8.

[115] Mohamed Sahnoun, *Somalia: Missed Opportunities* (Washington, DC: United States Institute of Peace Press, 1994), 25.

[116] In general, Aideed and other faction leaders were suspicious of Boutros-Ghali, who was believed to have been a strong supporter of the former Siad Barre regime. Shortly after Ismat Kittani replaced Sahnoun, relations became more antagonistic when the UN awarded contracting for operations of the Mogadishu airport to another clan (Hawadle). John Drysdale, "Foreign Military Intervention in Somalia," *Learning from Somalia: The Lessons of Armed Humanitarian Intervention*," edited by Walter Clarke and Jeffrey Herbst (Boulder, CO: Westview Press, 1997), 126.

[117] Andrew S. Natsios, "Humanitarian Relief Intervention in Somlia," in *Learning*, 83.

[118] Ken Menkhaus and Louis Ortmayer, "Key Decisions in the Somalia Intervention," *Pew Case Studies in International Relations* (Washington, DC: Institute for the Study of Diplomacy, Georgetown University, 1995), 3. See also Natsios, "Humanitarian," 89-92, and *Sahnoun*, Somalia, 35.

[119] Robert B. Oakley, "An Envoy„s Perspective," *Joint Force Quarterly* (Autumn 1993): 47.

[120] Rosegrant, "A „Seamless" Transition," 18.

[121] Ibid., 4.

[122] Menkhaus, "Key Decisions," 12.

[123] According to Oakley, "we would do our very best not to take sides, irrespective of who we liked and didn„t like. We were there to help Somalia. We weren„t there to impose something on them." Quoted in Rosegrant, "A „Seamless" Transition,"17.

[124] Ibid., 20.

[125] Ibid., 17.

[126] Ibid., 29.

[127] James Dobbins, John G. McGinn, Keith Crane, Seth G. Jones, Rollie Lal, Andrew Rathmell, Rachel M. Swanger, and Anga R. Timilsina, *America's Role in Nation-Building: From Germany to Iraq* (Santa Monica, CA: RAND Publications, 2002), 64.

[128] Rosegrant, "A „Seamless" Transition,"24.

[129] UNITAF conducted 986 airlift missions, moving 33,000 passengers and over 32,000 short tons of cargo. Eleven ships moved 365,000 tons and 1,192 supply containers. David D. Laitin, "Somalia Intervention in Internal Conflict," *Military Intervention: Cases in Context of the Twenty-First Century*, edited by William J. Lahneman (NY: Rowman & Littlefield Publishers, Inc., 2004), 36.

[130] Boutros-Ghali, "Introduction," 43.

[131] Nora Bensahel, "Somalia," in Art, *The United States*, 42

[132] Matthew Bryden, "Somalia: The Wages of Failure," *Current History* (April 1995): 150.

[133] Quoted in Rosengrant, "The „Seamless" Transition," 38.

[134] Dobbins, *America's Role*, 66.

---

[135] Art, "Coercive," 399.